Selected from

IN THE SHADOW
OF MAN

JANE GOODALL

Supplementary material by Edward Lavitt
and the staff of
Literacy Volunteers of New York City

WRITERS' VOICES
LITERACY VOLUNTEERS OF NEW YORK

WRITERS' VOICES™ was made possible by grants from: An anonymous foundation; The Vincent Astor Foundation; Exxon Corporation; Knight Foundation; Scripps Howard Foundation; Uris Brothers Foundation and H. W. Wilson Foundation.

ATTENTION READERS: We would like to hear what you think about our books. Please send your comments or suggestions to:

> The Editors
> Literacy Volunteers of New York City
> 121 Avenue of the Americas
> New York, NY 10013

Selection: From IN THE SHADOW OF MAN, revised edition, by Jane Goodall with photographs by Hugo Van Lawick, published by Houghton Mifflin Company, Boston. Copyright © 1971 by Jane Goodall and Hugo Van Lawick. Revisions copyright © 1988 by Jane Goodall. Reprinted by permission. Illustrations on pp. 31 and 44 are by David Bygott.

Supplementary materials © 1992 by Literacy Volunteers of New York City Inc.

Printed in the United States of America.

98 97 96 95 94 93 92 10 9 8 7 6 5 4 3 2 1

First LVNYC Printing: May 1992
ISBN 0-929631-52-8

Writers' Voices is a series of books published by Literacy Volunteers of New York City Inc., 121 Avenue of the Americas, New York, NY 10013. The words, "Writers' Voices," are a trademark of Literacy Volunteers of New York City.

Cover designed by Paul Davis Studio; interior designed by Jules Perlmutter/Off-Broadway Graphics.

Publishing Director, LVNYC: Nancy McCord
Managing Editor: Sarah Kirshner
Publishing Coordinator: Yvette Martinez-Gonzalez
Marketing and Production Manager: Elizabeth Bluemle

LVNYC is an affiliate of Literacy Volunteers of America.

Acknowledgments

Literacy Volunteers of New York City gratefully acknowledges the generous support of the following foundations and corporations that made the publication of WRITERS' VOICES and NEW WRITERS' VOICES possible: An anonymous foundation; The Vincent Astor Foundation; Exxon Corporation; Knight Foundation; Scripps Howard Foundation; Uris Brothers Foundation and H. W. Wilson Foundation.

This book could not have been realized without the kind and generous cooperation of the author, Jane Goodall, and her publisher, Houghton Mifflin Company. Thanks to Deborah Engel and Anne Harris, Subsidiary Rights.

We deeply appreciate the contributions of the following suppliers: Cam Steel Rule Die Works Inc. (steel cutting die for display); Domtar Industries Inc. (text stock); Westchester Book Composition (text typesetting); Horizon Paper Company (cover stock); MCUSA (display header); Delta Corrugated Container (corrugated display); Verilen Graphics Inc. (cover color separations); and Offset Paperback Manufacturers, Inc., A Bertelsmann Company (cover and text printing and binding).

For their guidance, support and hard work, we are indebted to the LVNYC Board of Directors' Publishing Committee: James E. Galton, Marvel Comics Ltd.; Virginia Barber, Virginia Barber Literary Agency, Inc.; Doris Bass, Scholastic Inc.; Jeff Brown; Jerry Butler, William Morrow & Company, Inc.; George P. Davidson, Ballantine Books; Joy M. Gannon, St. Martin's Press; Walter Kiechel, *Fortune*; Geraldine E. Rhoads; Virginia Rice, Reader's Digest; Martin Singerman, News America Publishing, Inc.; James L. Stanko, James Money Management, Inc. and F. Robert Stein, Pryor, Cashman, Sherman & Flynn.

Thanks also to Joy Gannon and Julia Weil of St. Martin's Press for producing this book; Virginia Barber for help in obtaining permissions; Edward Lavitt for his skill and diligence in the research and writing of the supplementary material for this book; Marlene Charnizon for her thoughtful copyediting and suggestions; and to Pam Johnson for proofreading. Thanks to Gillian D. Dundas and The Jane Goodall Institute for help in obtaining photos and to F. Robert Stein for legal advice.

Our thanks to Paul Davis Studio and Myrna Davis, Paul Davis, Lisa Mazur, Chalkley Calderwood and Alex Ginns for their inspired design of the covers of these books. Thanks also to Jules Perlmutter for his sensitive design of the interior of this book, and to AnneLouise Burns for design of maps and diagrams.

And finally, special credit must be given to Marilyn Boutwell, Jean Fargo and Gary Murphy of the LVNYC staff for their contributions to the educational and editorial content of these books.

Contents

Note
to the Reader

In the Shadow of Man is an autobiography. The author, Jane Goodall, writes about how she came to study the wild chimpanzees in Tanzania, Africa, and what she found there. Jane Goodall doesn't just write about her own life, though. She writes about the lives of the chimpanzees she observed. Studying animals and their habits in the wild is called natural science. Many people enjoy reading what natural scientists write about animals—it helps them understand the links and differences between human beings and animals.

Every writer has a special voice. That is why we call our series Writers' Voices. We chose In the Shadow of Man because Jane Goodall's voice can be clearly heard as she tells her thoughts and discoveries while studying the chimpanzees. In choosing parts from the book, we wanted you to hear how Jane Goodall worked to study something she felt passionate about, in spite of her lack of formal training.

In addition to the selections themselves, this book has several other chapters. They provide background information that can help you in understanding the selections. You may choose to read some or all of these chapters before or after reading the selections.

- Reading "About the Selections from *In the Shadow of Man*" on page 10 will help you to begin thinking about what you will read in the selections.
- If you would like more information about chimpanzees and their animal relatives, look at the chapter called "About Primates: Gorillas and Chimpanzees" on page 56.
- In the chapter "About Jane Goodall," on page 53, you will find information about the author that is not in the selections from her autobiography. Sometimes this information will give you more insight into the selections.

If you are a new reader, you may want to have this book read aloud to you, perhaps more than once. Even if you are a more experienced reader, you may enjoy hearing it read aloud before reading it silently to yourself.

We encourage you to read *actively*. Here are some things you can do.

Before Reading

- Read the front and back covers of the book, and look at the cover illustration. Ask yourself what you expect the book to be about.
- Think about why you want to read this book. Perhaps you have seen one of Jane Goodall's *National Geographic* specials on TV. Maybe you enjoy learning about animals.
- Look at the Contents page. See where you can find a map of places mentioned in the selections and other information. Decide what you want to read and in what order.

During Reading

- There may be words that natural scientists use or other words that are difficult to read. Keep reading to see if the meaning becomes clear. If it doesn't, ask someone for the meaning of the word. Some of the words may be in the glossary on page 46. Or look up the word in a dictionary.
- Ask yourself questions as you read. For example: How would it feel to be in the forest studying shy, wild animals?

After Reading

- Think about what you have read. Did you identify with Jane Goodall or her experiences? Did they make you see any of your own experiences in a new light?
- Talk with others about your thoughts.
- Try some of the questions and activities in "Questions for the Reader" on page 49. They are meant to help you discover more about what you have read and how it relates to you.

The editors of *Writers' Voices* hope you will write to us. We want to know your thoughts about our books.

About the Selections from IN THE SHADOW OF MAN

On July 16, 1960, Jane Goodall, a 26-year-old former secretary from England, began to study the behavior of chimpanzees in the wild. Until that time, scientists had mostly observed and studied chimpanzees in laboratories and zoos. Few scientists had gone to the remote areas in Africa where the chimps live to study them. When they had studied the chimps in the wild, they hadn't spent long periods of time observing them. Jane Goodall planned to watch the chimps in Africa over ten years and see exactly how they behaved. She was not a professional scientist when she started out. *In the Shadow of Man* tells how she began her project and what she discovered.

As Goodall said in 1973, "I had no qualifications at all. I was just somebody with a love of animals." Her love of animals drew her to

Africa where she met Dr. Louis S. B. Leakey. Leakey was a world-famous scientist who was studying how prehistoric man lived. Since chimps are man's closest living relatives, Leakey thought prehistoric man might have lived in the same ways the chimps live today. Leakey told Goodall that studying chimps might give clues about the way early man lived.

Leakey asked Goodall to study the chimpanzees at Gombe on the shores of Lake Tanganyika in Tanzania, Africa. The chimps were very shy and the country was very rugged. Goodall took on the difficult job of finding and watching the chimps.

The selections from *In the Shadow of Man* start out by telling about the first time the chimps let Goodall come close to them and how this made her feel. Goodall then tells how she began her project and why Dr. Leakey thought she might be good at it even though she was not a trained scientist. She tells how she felt when she first saw the rugged country she would have to enter to study the chimps. And, finally she tells about what she discovered after watching the chimps carefully for months.

The things Jane Goodall discovered changed

scientists' and others' views of chimps and their relationship to man. Even though she had no special training, Jane Goodall taught herself to be a good observer and to keep careful records of what she saw. The selections from her book, *In the Shadow of Man*, tell how she began what turned into more than 30 years of studying animals in Africa.

Perhaps these selections will make you think about different ways of observing the world around you. Or they may remind you of how it feels to do something that you've always wanted to do.

Selected from
IN THE SHADOW
OF MAN

JANE GOODALL

1 / Beginnings

Since dawn I had climbed up and down the steep mountain slopes and pushed my way through the dense valley forests. Again and again I had stopped to listen, or to gaze through binoculars at the surrounding countryside. Yet I had neither heard nor seen a single chimpanzee, and now it was already five o'clock. In two hours darkness would fall over the rugged terrain of the Gombe Stream Chimpanzee Reserve. I settled down at my favorite vantage point, the Peak, hoping that at least I might see a chimpanzee make his nest for the night before I had to stop work for the day.

I was watching a troop of monkeys in the forested valley below when suddenly I heard the screaming of a young chimpanzee. Quickly

I scanned the trees with my binoculars, but the sound had died away before I could locate the exact place, and it took several minutes of searching before I saw four chimpanzees. The slight squabble was over and they were all feeding peacefully on some yellow plumlike fruits.

The distance between us was too great for me to make detailed observations, so I decided to try to get closer. I surveyed the trees close to the group: if I could manage to get to that large fig without frightening the chimpanzees, I thought, I would get an excellent view. It took me about ten minutes to make the journey. As I moved cautiously around the thick gnarled trunk of the fig I realized that the chimpanzees had gone; the branches of the fruit tree were empty. The same old feeling of depression clawed at me. Once again the chimpanzees had seen me and silently fled. Then all at once my heart missed several beats.

Less than twenty yards away from me two male chimpanzees were sitting on the ground staring at me intently. Scarcely breathing, I waited for the sudden panic-stricken flight that normally followed a surprise encounter between myself and the chimpanzees at close quarters.

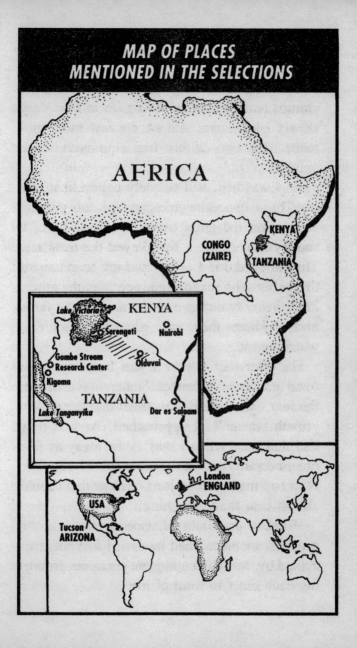

MAP OF PLACES
MENTIONED IN THE SELECTIONS

AFRICA

CONGO
(ZAIRE)

KENYA

TANZANIA

Lake Victoria

KENYA

Serengeti

Nairobi

Gombe Stream
Research Center

Olduvai

Kigoma

TANZANIA

Lake Tanganyika

Dar es Salaam

London
ENGLAND

USA

Tucson
ARIZONA

But nothing of the sort happened. The two large chimps simply continued to gaze at me. Very slowly I sat down, and after a few more moments, the two calmly began to groom one another.

As I watched, still scarcely believing it was true, I saw two more chimpanzee heads peering at me over the grass from the other side of a small forest glade: a female and a youngster. They bobbed down as I turned my head toward them, but soon reappeared, one after the other, in the lower branches of a tree about forty yards away. There they sat, almost motionless, watching me.

For over half a year I had been trying to overcome the chimpanzees' inherent fear of me, the fear that made them vanish into the undergrowth whenever I approached. At first they had fled even when I was as far away as five hundred yards and on the other side of a ravine. Now two males were sitting so close that I could almost hear them breathing.

Without any doubt whatsoever, this was the proudest moment I had known. I had been accepted by the two magnificent creatures grooming each other in front of me.

It had all begun three years before [1957] when I had met Dr. L. S. B. Leakey, the well-known anthropologist and paleontologist, in Nairobi. Or perhaps it had begun in my earliest childhood. When I was just over one year old my mother gave me a toy chimpanzee, a large hairy model celebrating the birth of the first chimpanzee infant ever born in the London zoo. Most of my mother's friends were horrified and predicted that the ghastly creature would give a small child nightmares; but Jubilee (as the celebrated infant itself was named) was my most loved possession and accompanied me on all my childhood travels. I still have the worn old toy.

Quite apart from Jubilee, I had been fascinated by live animals from the time when I first learned to crawl. One of my earliest recollections is of the day that I hid in a small stuffy henhouse in order to see how a hen laid an egg. I emerged after about five hours. The whole household had apparently been searching for me for hours, and my mother had even rung the police to report me missing.

It was about four years later, when I was eight, that I first decided I would go to Africa and live with wild animals when I grew up. Although when I left school at eighteen I took a secretarial course and then two different jobs, the longing for Africa was still very much with me. So much so that when I received an invitation to go and stay with a school friend at her parents' farm in Kenya I handed in my resignation the same day and left a fascinating job at a documentary film studio.

"If you are interested in animals," someone said to me about a month after my arrival in Africa, "then you should meet Dr. Leakey." I had already started on a somewhat dreary office job, since I had not wanted to overstay my welcome at my friend's farm. I went to see Louis Leakey at what is now the National Museum of natural history in Nairobi, where at that same time he was Curator. Somehow he must have sensed that my interest in animals was not just a passing phase, but was rooted deep, for on the spot he gave me a job as an assistant secretary.

I learned much while working at the museum. The staff all were keen naturalists full of enthusiasm and were happy to share some of their boundless knowledge with me. Best of all, I was offered the chance, with one other girl, of accompanying Dr. Leakey and his wife Mary on one of their annual paleontological expeditions to Olduvai Gorge on the Serengeti plains.

Toward the end of our time at Olduvai Louis Leakey began to talk to me about a group of chimpanzees living on the shores of Lake Tanganyika. The chimpanzee is found only in Africa, where it ranges across the equatorial forest belt from the west coast to a point just east of Lake Tanganyika. The group Louis was referring to comprised chimpanzees of the Eastern or Long-haired variety. Louis described their habitat as mountainous, rugged, and completely cut off from civilization. He spoke for a while of the dedication and patience that would be required of any person who tried to study them.

Much more Louis told me during that first talk. He was, he said, particularly interested in the behavior of a group of chimpanzees living on the shores of a lake—for the remains of prehistoric man were often found on a lakeshore and it was possible that an understanding of chimpanzee behavior today might shed light on the behavior of our stone age ancestors.

I could hardly believe that he spoke seriously when, after a pause, he asked me if I would be willing to tackle the job. Although it was the sort of thing I most wanted to do, I was not qualified to undertake a scientific study of animal behavior. Louis, however, knew exactly what he was doing. Not only did he feel that a university training was unnecessary, but even that in some ways it might have been disadvantageous. He wanted someone with a mind uncluttered and unbiased by theory who would make the study for no other reason than a real desire for knowledge; and, in addition, someone with a sympathetic understanding of animals.

Goodall was delighted and agreed to take on the job. There were several problems to solve before she could actually start her fieldwork. First, Leakey had to find the money for Goodall to start the project. Since the area where she was to study the chimpanzees was remote, she would need a tent, a small boat to travel on the nearby lake and airfare from England. (Goodall had to return home first.)

The local government in Kigoma told Good-

all that she must have a European companion with her when she worked in the forest.

Leakey was able to get money for the project, and Goodall's mother, Vanne Goodall, agreed to go with her while she studied the chimps.

Early in 1960, Goodall and her mother arrived in Nairobi ready to leave for Kigoma to start her research. There they were told that they would have to wait because there was some trouble among the African fishermen on the beaches of the chimpanzee reserve. Leakey suggested that Goodall make a short trial study of a group of vervet monkeys (a common African monkey) on an island in Lake Victoria.

The study of the monkeys turned out to be good practice for the later chimpanzee project. Then, after three weeks, the Goodalls received word that they could go on to Kigoma and the reserve at Gombe Stream. The 800-mile overland trip in a Land Rover took three days, and when they arrived, they found out that there had been some violence in the Congo, 25 miles across Lake Tanganyika.

This created another setback. The local government was afraid that the violence across the lake might have spilled over to the Gombe area,

*and they would not let the Goodalls go on to
the chimp area until they felt it was safe to work
there.*

*Finally, after a week, the Goodalls got the
go-ahead and they were allowed to leave for
Gombe. They traveled with David Anstey, the
Game Ranger for the reserve.*

2 / Early Days

I retained the strange feeling that I was living
in a dream world throughout the twelve-mile
journey from Kigoma to our camping place in
the Gombe Stream Chimpanzee Reserve. It was
the middle of the dry season, and the shoreline
of the Congo, though it was only some twenty-
five miles distant, was not even faintly dis-
cernible to the west of long, narrow Lake Tanganyika. The fresh breeze and the deep blue of
the water, choppy with small waves and flecked
with white foam, combined to make us feel that
we were at sea.

I gazed at the eastern shoreline. Between Kigoma and the start of the chimpanzee sanctuary
the steep slopes of the rift escarpment, which
rise twenty-five hundred feet above the lake,

are in many places bare and eroded from years of tree felling. In between, small pockets of forest cling to the narrow valleys where fast-flowing mountain streams rush down to the lake. The coastline is broken into a series of elongated bays often separated by rocky head-lands that jut out into the lake. We steered a straight course, proceeding from headland to headland and noticing that the little canoes of the fishermen hugged the shoreline. David Anstey, who was traveling with us to introduce us to the local African inhabitants of the area, explained that sometimes the lake becomes suddenly rough, with fierce winds sweeping down the valleys and churning the water into a welter of spray and waves.

All along the shoreline fishing villages clung to the mountain slopes or nestled in the mouths of the valleys. The dwellings were mostly simple mud and grass huts, although even in those days there were a few larger buildings roofed with shiny corrugated iron—that curse, for those who love natural beauty, of the modern African landscape.

When we had traveled about seven miles, David pointed out the large rocky outcrop mark-

ing the southern limits of the chimpanzee reserve. Once past the boundary we noticed that
the country changed suddenly and dramatically:
here the mountains were thickly wooded and
intersected by valleys supporting dense tropical
forests.

Since that day I have often wondered exactly
what it was I felt as I stared at the wild country
that so soon I should be roaming. Vanne ad-
mitted afterward to have been secretly horrified
by the steepness of the slopes and the impenetrable appearance of the valley forests. And
David Anstey told me several months later that
he had guessed I would be packed up and gone
within six weeks. I remember feeling neither
excitement nor trepidation but only a curious
sense of detachment. What had I, the girl standing on the government launch in her jeans, to
do with the girl who in a few days would be
searching those very mountains for wild
chimpanzees?

The next morning, though I was eager to go
out looking for chimpanzees, I soon found that
to start with, anyway, I was not to be my own
master. David Anstey had arranged for a number of the local Africans to come and meet

Vanne and me. He explained that they were all worried and resentful; they could not believe a young girl would come all the way from England just to look at apes, and so the rumor had spread that I was a government spy. Naturally I was very grateful to David for sorting things out for me right at the start, but my heart sank when I heard the plans he had made for me.

First it was agreed that the son of the chief of Mwamgongo, a large fishing village to the north of the chimpanzee reserve, should accompany me. He would make sure that when I saw one chimpanzee I did not write down in my book that I had seen ten or twenty. Later I realized that the Africans were still hoping to reclaim the thirty square miles of the reserve for themselves: if I stated that there were more chimpanzees than in fact there were, the Africans felt the government could then make a better case for keeping the area a protected reserve. Second, David felt that for the sake of my prestige I should employ an African to carry my haversack.

Since I was convinced the only way to establish contact with shy animals was to move about alone, I was upset to think I must be encumbered by two companions.

Goodall and her two African companions, Rashidi and Adolf, started to look for chimpanzees in the forests of the reserve. For the first two months of her project, Goodall only saw glimpses of the chimps from far away. When she tried to get closer, the chimps ran off.

In between the disappointing days, when we only saw chimps too far off to observe properly or for a few minutes close by before they fled, were even worse days when we saw no chimps at all. The more I thought of the task I had set myself, the more despondent I became. Nevertheless, those weeks did serve to acquaint me with the rugged terrain. My skin became hardened to the rough grasses of the valleys and my blood immune to the poison of the tsetse fly, so that I no longer swelled hugely each time I was bitten. I became increasingly surefooted on the treacherous slopes, which were equally slippery whether they were bare and eroded, crusted with charcoal, or carpeted by dry, trampled grass. Gradually, too, I became familiar with many of the animal tracks in the five valleys that became my main work area.

I encountered many of the other denizens of the mountains during our daily wanderings: huge gray bushpigs with their silvery spinal crests; groups of banded mongooses rustling through the leaves in search of insects; the squirrels and the striped and spotted elephant shrews of the thick forests. Gradually, too, I sorted out the many different kinds of monkeys that can be found in the Gombe Stream area.

Rashidi taught me a great deal about bush lore, and how to find my way through seemingly impenetrable forest. Despite my initial disappointment when I had heard that I was not allowed to be alone, I was grateful for his help during those early days. Soon he had to leave me, to return for a while to his village. Since I found that Adolf the scout was not suited to long arduous hours in the mountains without food, I had a succession of other African companions during the next few months. There was Soko, from Nyanza, whose name caused much amusement among the local Africans, for this is their word for chimpanzee. Next came the enormously tall and willowy Wilbert, who always looked immaculate even after scrambling on his belly along a pig trail; and finally Short, who, as his name implies, was very small. All three were tough men who had spent their lives working in the bush with animals, and I enjoyed their company and learned much during the days they worked for me.

3 / First Observations

About three months after our arrival, Vanne and I fell ill at the same time. It was undoubtedly some sort of malaria, but since we had been told by no lesser person than the doctor in Kigoma that there was no malaria in the area we had no drugs with us. How he came to believe such a strange fallacy I cannot imagine. We were too naive to question him at that time. For nearly two weeks we lay side by side on our low camp beds in our hot, stuffy tent sweating out the fever.

As soon as the fever left me I was impatient to start work again. Nearly three months had sped away, and I felt that I had learned nothing.

I was frantic—in a couple of months my funds would run out. I could not bear the thought of any of my African companions seeing me in my weak state and so, risking official displeasure, I set off alone one morning for the mountain I had climbed on my first afternoon—the mountain that rose directly above our camp. I left at my usual time, when it was still cool, in the first glimmerings of dawn. After ten minutes or so my heart began to hammer wildly, I could feel the blood pounding in my head, and I had to stop to catch my breath. Eventually I reached an open peak about one thousand feet above the lake. It offered a superb view over the home valley, so I decided to sit there for a while and search for signs of chimpanzees through my binoculars.

I had been there some fifteen minutes when a slight movement on the bare burned slope just beyond a narrow ravine caught my eye. I looked around and saw three chimps standing there staring at me. I expected them to flee, for they were no farther than eighty yards away, but after a moment they moved on again, quite calmly, and were soon lost to sight in some thicker vegetation. Had I been correct, after all, in my assumption that they would be less afraid of one person completely alone? For even when I had left my African companions behind and approached a group on my own, the chimps had undoubtedly been fully aware of what was going on.

I remained on my peak, and later on in the morning a group of chimps, with much screaming and barking and pant-hooting, careered down the opposite mountain slope and began feeding in some fig trees that grew thickly along the streambanks in the valley below me. They had only been there about twenty minutes when another procession of chimps crossed the bare slope where earlier I had seen the three. This group also saw me since I was very conspicuous on the rocky peak. Although they all stopped and stared and then hastened their steps slightly as they moved on again, the chimpanzees did not run in panic. Presently, with violent swaying of branches and wild calling, this group joined the chimpanzees already feeding on figs. After a time they settled down to feed quietly together, and when they finally climbed down from the trees they moved off in one big group. For part of the way, as they walked up the

Hoo part of pant-hoot.   *Waa* part of pant-hoot.

This is how a chimpanzee's face looks when it *pant-hoots*. Chimpanzees make these calls to each other when they find food, join a group or a group is moving from one place to another.

Jane Goodall watches chimps play on the shores of Lake Tanganyika.

valley, I could see them following each other in a long, orderly line. Two small infants were perched like jockeys on their mothers' backs. I even saw them pause to drink, each one for about a minute, before leaping across the stream.

It was by far the best day I had had since my arrival at Gombe, and when I got back to camp that evening I was exhilarated, if exhausted. Vanne, who had been far more ill than I and was still in bed, was much cheered by my excitement.

That day, in fact, marked the turning point in my study. The fig trees grow all along the lower reaches of the stream and that year the crop in our valley was plentiful, lasting for eight weeks. Every day I returned to my peak, and every day chimpanzees fed on the figs below. They came in large groups and small groups, singly and in pairs. Regularly they passed me, either moving along the original route across the open slope just above me or along one or other of the trails crossing the grassy ridge below me. And because I always looked the same, wearing similar dull-colored clothes, and never tried to follow them or harass them in any way, the shy chimpanzees began to realize, at long last, that after all I was not so horrific and terrifying. Also, I was usually alone on my peak; there was no need for my African companions to follow me up and down, since they knew where I was going to be. When Short had to leave I decided to employ no other African, and although Adolf and afterward Saulo David, the new scout, often came up in the evenings to make sure I was all right, mostly I was completely on my own.

My peak quickly became the Peak. It is, I think, the very best vantage point for watching chimpanzees in the whole of the Gombe Stream sanctuary.

I carried a small tin trunk up to the Peak and there kept a kettle, some coffee, a few tins of baked beans, a sweater, and a blanket. A tiny stream trickled through Buffalo Wood. It was almost nonexistent in the dry season, but I scooped out a shallow bowl in the gravelly streambed and so was able to collect enough of the sparkling clear water for my needs. When the chimpanzees slept near the Peak I often stayed up there too—then I didn't have to trudge up the mountain in the morning. I was able to send messages down to Vanne with whichever of the Game Scouts climbed to the Peak in the evening so that she always knew when I was planning to stay out for the night.

For about a month I spent most of each day either on the Peak or overlooking Mlinda Valley where the chimps, before or after stuffing themselves with figs, ate large quantities of small purple fruits that tasted, like so many of their foods, as bitter and astringent as sloes or crab apples. Piece by piece, I began to form my first somewhat crude picture of chimpanzee life.

While many details of their social behavior were hidden from me by the foliage, I did get occasional fascinating glimpses. I saw one female, newly arrived in a group, hurry up to a big male and hold her hand toward him. Almost regally he reached out, clasped her hand in his, drew it toward him, and kissed it with his lips. I saw two adult males embrace each other in greeting. I saw youngsters having wild games through the treetops, chasing around after each other or jumping again and again, one after the other, from a branch to a springy bough below. I watched small infants dangling happily by themselves for minutes on end, patting at their toes with one hand, rotating gently from side to side. Once two tiny infants pulled on opposite ends of a twig in a gentle tug-of-war. Often, during the heat of midday or after a long spell of feeding, I saw two or more adults grooming each other, carefully looking through the hair of their companions.

At that time of year the chimps usually went to bed late, making their nests when it was too dark to see properly through binoculars, but sometimes they nested earlier and I could watch them from the Peak. I found that every individual, except for infants who slept with their mothers, made his own nest each night. Generally this took about three minutes: the chimp chose a firm foundation such as an upright fork or crotch, or two horizontal branches. Then he reached out and bent over smaller branches onto this foundation, keeping each one in place with his feet. Finally he tucked in the small leafy twigs growing around the rim of his nest and lay down. Quite often a chimp sat up after a few minutes and picked a handful of leafy twigs, which he put under his head or some other part of his body before settling down again for the night. One young female I watched went

on and on bending down branches until she had
constructed a huge mound of greenery on which
she finally curled up.

I climbed up into some of the nests after the
chimpanzees had left them. Most of them were
built in trees that for me were almost impossible
to climb. I found that there was quite compli-
cated interweaving of the branches in some of
them. I found, too, that the nests were never
fouled with dung; and later, when I was able
to get closer to the chimps, I saw how they
were always careful to defecate and urinate over
the edge of their nests, even in the middle of
the night.

As the weeks went by the chimpanzees became less and less afraid. Quite often when I
was on one of my food-collecting expeditions
I came across chimpanzees unexpectedly, and
after a time I found that some of them would
tolerate my presence provided they were in
fairly thick forest and I sat still and did not try
to move closer than sixty to eighty yards. And
so, during my second month of watching from
the Peak, when I saw a group settle down to
feed I sometimes moved closer and was thus
able to make more detailed observations.

It was at this time that I began to recognize a number of different individuals. As soon as I was sure of knowing a chimpanzee if I saw it again, I named it. Some scientists feel that animals should be labeled by numbers—that to name them is anthropomorphic—but I have always been interested in the *differences* between individuals, and a name is not only more individual than a number but also far easier to remember. Most names were simply those which, for some reason or other, seemed to suit the individuals to whom I attached them. A few chimps were named because some facial expression or mannerism reminded me of human acquaintances.

Two of the chimpanzees I knew well by sight at that time were David Graybeard and Goliath. Like David and Goliath in the Bible, these two individuals were closely associated in my mind because they were very often together. Goliath, even in those days of his prime, was not a giant, but he had a splendid physique and the springy movements of an athlete. He probably weighed about one hundred pounds. David Graybeard was less afraid of me from the start than were any of the other chimps. I was always pleased when I picked out his handsome face and well-marked silvery beard in a chimpanzee group, for with David to calm the others, I had a better chance of approaching to observe them more closely.

Before the end of my trial period in the field I made two really exciting discoveries—discoveries that made the previous months of frustration well worth while. And for both of them I had David Graybeard to thank.

One day I arrived on the Peak and found a small group of chimps just below me in the upper branches of a thick tree. As I watched I saw that one of them was holding a pink-looking object from which he was from time to time pulling pieces with his teeth. There was a female and a youngster and they were both reaching out toward the male, their hands actually touching his mouth. Presently the female picked up a piece of the pink thing and put it to her mouth: it was at this moment that I realized the chimps were eating meat.

After each bite of meat the male picked off some leaves with his lips and chewed them with the flesh. Often, when he had chewed for several minutes on this leafy wad, he spat out the remains into the waiting hands of the female. Suddenly he dropped a small piece of meat, and like a flash the youngster swung after it to the ground. Even as he reached to pick it up the undergrowth exploded and an adult bushpig charged toward him. Screaming, the juvenile leaped back into the tree. The pig remained in the open, snorting and moving backward and forward. Soon I made out the shapes of three small striped piglets. Obviously the chimps were eating a baby pig. The size was right and later, when I realized that the male was David Graybeard, I moved closer and saw that he was indeed eating piglet.

For three hours I watched the chimps feeding. David occasionally let the female bite pieces from the carcass and once he actually detached a small piece of flesh and placed it in her outstretched hand. When he finally climbed down there was still meat left on the carcass; he carried it away in one hand, followed by the others.

Of course I was not sure, then, that David Graybeard had caught the pig for himself, but even so, it was tremendously exciting to know that these chimpanzees actually ate meat. Previously scientists had believed that although these apes might occasionally supplement their diet with a few insects or small rodents and the like they were primarily vegetarians and fruit eaters. No one had suspected that they might hunt larger mammals.

It was within two weeks of this observation that I saw something that excited me even more. By then it was October and the short rains had begun. The blackened slopes were softened by feathery new grass shoots and in some places the ground was carpeted by a variety of flowers. The Chimpanzees' Spring, I called it. I had had a frustrating morning, tramping up and down three valleys with never a sign or sound of a chimpanzee. Hauling myself up the steep slope of Mlinda Valley I headed for the Peak, not only weary but soaking wet from crawling through dense undergrowth. Suddenly I stopped, for I saw a slight movement in the long grass about sixty yards away. Quickly focusing my binoculars I saw that it was a single chimpanzee, and just then he turned in my direction. I recognized David Graybeard.

Cautiously I moved around so that I could see what he was doing. He was squatting beside the red earth mound of a termite nest, and as I watched I saw him carefully push a long grass stem down into a hole in the mound. After a moment he withdrew it and picked something from the end with his mouth. I was too far away to make out what he was eating, but it was obvious that he was actually using a grass stem as a tool.

I knew that on two occasions casual observers in West Africa had seen chimpanzees using objects as tools: one had broken open palm-nut kernels by using a rock as a hammer, and a group of chimps had been observed pushing sticks into an underground bees' nest and licking off the honey. Somehow I had never dreamed of seeing anything so exciting myself.

For an hour David feasted at the termite mound and then he wandered slowly away. When I was sure he had gone I went over to examine the mound. I found a few crushed insects strewn about, and a swarm of worker termites sealing the entrances of the nest passages into which David had obviously been poking his stems. I picked up one of his discarded tools and carefully pushed it into a hole myself. Immediately I felt the pull of several termites as they seized the grass, and when I pulled it out there were a number of worker termites and a few soldiers, with big red heads, clinging on with their mandibles. There they remained, sticking out at right angles to the stem with their legs waving in the air.

Before I left I trampled down some of the tall dry grass and constructed a rough hide— just a few palm fronds leaned up against the low branch of a tree and tied together at the top. I planned to wait there the next day. But it was another week before I was able to watch a chimpanzee "fishing" for termites again. Twice chimps arrived, but each time they saw me and moved off immediately. Once a swarm of fertile winged termites—the princes and princesses, as they are called—flew off on their nuptial flight, their huge white wings fluttering frantically as they carried the insects higher and higher. Later I realized that it is at this time of year, during the short rains, when the worker termites extend the passages of the nest to the surface, preparing for these emigrations. Several such swarms emerge between October and January. It is principally during these months that the chimpanzees feed on termites.

On the eighth day of my watch David Gray-beard arrived again, together with Goliath, and the pair worked there for two hours. I could see much better: I observed how they scratched open the sealed-over passage entrances with a thumb or forefinger. I watched how they bit the ends off their tools when they became bent, or used the other end, or discarded them in favor of new ones. Goliath once moved at least fifteen yards from the heap to select a firm-looking piece of vine, and both males often picked three or four stems while they were collecting tools, and put the spares beside them on the ground until they wanted them.

Most exciting of all, on several occasions they picked small leafy twigs and prepared them for use by stripping off the leaves. This was the first recorded example of a wild animal not merely *using* an object as a tool, but actually modifying an object and thus showing the crude beginnings of tool*making*.

Previously man had been regarded as the only tool-making animal. Indeed, one of the clauses commonly accepted in the definition of man was that he was a creature who "made tools to a regular and set pattern." The chimpanzees,

These chimpanzees use grass stems to "fish" a termite mound for termites. They strip the leaves from a stem to make a tool.

obviously, had not made tools to any set pattern. Nevertheless, my early observations of their primitive toolmaking abilities convinced a number of scientists that it was necessary to redefine man in a more complex manner than before. Or else, as Louis Leakey put it, we should by definition have to accept the chimpanzee as Man.

Note

Glossary

anthropologist. A scientist who studies human beings.

anthropomorphic. Crediting human traits to non-humans.

corrugated iron. A sheet of thin steel pressed into straight ridges and grooves to keep it stiff.

curator. A person in charge of a museum, zoo or similar exhibition place or a section of it.

equatorial. A region around the earth halfway between the North Pole and the South Pole. The climate is usually very hot all year long.

fossil. The remains of a plant or animal preserved in the earth.

habitat. A place where a plant or an animal is usually found.

haversack. A bag, usually worn over one shoulder, for carrying belongings or food on a march or hike.

lemur. A squirrel-like animal related to the monkey.

malaria. A disease spread by the bite of a certain kind of mosquito.

mammal. An animal whose young are fed mother's milk from her breast.

mandible. A jaw.

mongoose. A small, meat-eating mammal.

naturalist. A student of nature.

paleontologist. A scientist who studies fossils.

physique. The form of a body.

prehistoric. About the time in history before people recorded events in writing.

primates. Animals, such as apes, gorillas, baboons, chimpanzees and monkeys. Human beings are also primates.

reserve. Land set aside for a special purpose.

rift escarpment. A kind of cliff overlooking a place where the ground has been worn away. The walls of the cliff provide good hunting for fossils.

rodents. Small mammals that chew with a pair of front teeth resembling chisels. Rats, mice, squirrels and beavers are rodents.

sanctuary. A place where wildlife is protected from hunters.

shrews. Small mammals with pointed snouts and velvet-like fur. They usually sleep during the day and hunt for food at night.

sloe. A small, dark plum-like fruit.

stone age. The time of the earliest known human beings. These prehistoric people used stone tools.

termite. An ant-like insect that feeds on wood.

tsetse. [SET-see] A small fly that carries a tiny germ-like, one-celled animal that causes sleeping sickness.

Questions for the Reader

Thinking about the Story

1. What was interesting for you about the selections from *In the Shadow of Man?*

2. Did the events or people in the selections became important or special to you in some way? Write about or discuss your thoughts.

3. What do you think were the most important things Jane Goodall wanted to say in the selections?

4. In what ways did the selections answer the questions you had before you began reading or listening?

5. Were any parts of the selections difficult to understand? If so, you may want to read or listen to them again. Discuss with your learning partners possible reasons why they were difficult.

Activities

1. Were there any words that were difficult for you in the selections from *In the Shadow of Man*? Go back to these words and try to figure out their meanings. Discuss what you think each word means, and why you made that guess. Look them up in a dictionary and see if your definitions are the same or different.

   Discuss with your learning partners how you are going to remember each word. Some ways to remember words are to put them on file cards, write them in a journal or create a personal dictionary. Be sure to use the words in your writing in a way that will help you remember their meanings.

2. Talking with other people about what you have read can increase your understanding. Discussion can help you organize your thoughts, get new ideas and rethink your original ideas. Discuss your thoughts about the selections from *In the Shadow of Man* with someone else who has read them. Find out if you helped yourself understand the

selections in the same or different ways. Find out if your opinions about the selections are the same or different. See if your thoughts change as a result of this discussion.

3. After you finish reading or listening, you might want to write down your thoughts about the book. You could write your reflections on the book in a journal, or you could write about topics the book has brought up that you want to explore further. You could write a book review or a letter to a friend who you think might be interested in the book.

4. Did reading the selections give you any ideas for your own writing? You might want to write about:

- a job or project you have dreamed about doing.

- a discovery you have made by closely watching some special person, place or thing.

- starting out on an adventure.

5. Jane Goodall kept careful notes about what she observed. You might try writing notes or tape-recording your observations about things you see. After you have made your observations, look over or listen to your notes and try writing a description of what you saw so someone else can picture it.

6. You might like to interview someone you think has an interesting job or career. How did they get started? What kind of training did they have? What did they learn on their own?

7. If you could talk to Jane Goodall, what questions would you ask about her work or her writing? You might want to write the questions in a journal.

About Jane Goodall

"Jane Goodall eats bugs." This tells a lot about how Goodall works to learn everything possible about the animals she studies. Since chimps eat termites, she ate some to find out what a chimp's diet tasted like. Goodall has always been very curious about the ways animals live.

Jane Goodall was born in England in 1934. When she was small, she spent a lot of time observing local animals. She dreamed of going to Africa to study animals in the wild and write about them. She left school at 18 and worked as a secretary until she had saved enough money to go to Africa. The result of that trip was a 30-year career as an animal researcher.

Some of the important things that Goodall saw and wrote about were the ways chimps behave in groups. She saw them hugging, cuddling, playing and fighting in ways that she thought were surprisingly similar to humans. She also saw chimps eat the meat of a baby pig (something that scientists had not observed before) and make and use very simple tools.

Now the small game reserve where she started observing the chimps has become Gombe National Park. Her camp has become the Gombe Stream Research Centre, with a large staff of local Africans working there. Jane Goodall has written five books and appeared in *National Geographic* television specials about her work. She is one of the best-known animal researchers in the world. She has been married twice and she has one son.

Goodall gives lectures about her work. She gives workshops to medical people who use chimps, monkeys and other primates for experiments. She tells them what she has learned about the animals and how scientists can improve the chimps' well-being in the laboratories.

Goodall also spends time in Africa supervising the scientists who have come to the Gombe Stream Research Centre. There she and others continue to study the chimps' way of life.

Another part of her time is spent with The Jane Goodall Institute in Tucson, Arizona. The institute has several functions. It helps to pay for the continuing research at Gombe and in other parts of Africa. It also helps scientists study chimps in zoos and laboratories. The institute works with groups throughout the world that promote the preservation of all wildlife.

Goodall's home base is in Dar es Salaam, Tanzania, where she spends time writing and answering letters. She also visits with officials of different African countries where primates are being studied in the wild. Permission to work in these places is not easy to obtain, so her visits help smooth the way for the work to continue. For relaxation, she enjoys reading mystery stories.

In spite of her busy life, she still enjoys going out in the field to watch animals. "Living under the skies," she says, "the forest is for me a temple, a cathedral made of tree canopies and dancing light, especially when it's raining and quiet. That's heaven on earth to me. I can't imagine going through life without being tuned in to the mystical side of nature."

About Primates: Gorillas and Chimpanzees

If you've ever gone to the zoo, you may have noticed how much apes, chimpanzees, monkeys and other monkey-like animals look like each other. Of all the animals, these creatures also resemble people the most. Their eyes are on the front of their heads, they sometimes walk upright on two legs and their hands look like our hands. In fact, these monkeys and monkey-like animals and human beings do have something in common. They are both primates.

Scientists group all living things into different categories or "families," depending on how much they are alike or different. Primates are one category of living creatures. Birds, snakes, dogs and elephants each belong to their own categories. Some differences between primates and other animals are obvious. Chimps and people do not have wings or beaks, for example. What do all primates have in common that makes them part of the same group?

- Primates (except for humans) live in trees.
- They have a thumb that is opposite their other fingers. The thumb allows them to grasp tree branches and other objects. (Think of other animals with paws or hooves. They aren't able to hold things the way primates do.)
- Almost all primates can sit or walk upright easily.
- Their brains are much more elaborate and developed than any other animal's.
- Most primates have a varied diet: leaves, berries, fruits, nuts, insects and animal flesh. They have several kinds of teeth so that they can chew a variety of food. Some teeth are for cutting (leaves, for example), some are for piercing and tearing (animal flesh) and some are for crushing and grinding (nuts and insects).

There are hundreds of different kinds of primates. Some of the most familiar are gorillas, chimpanzees, baboons and monkeys. Primates vary in size, weight and the places they live, or their habitat.

Gorillas

Gorillas are the largest primates of all. They can be as much as seven feet tall, and the distance between their outstretched arms can sometimes reach nine feet. In the wild, male gorillas weigh up to 600 pounds. In zoos, because they get much less exercise, they can weigh as much as 800 pounds.

In spite of their fierce look, gorillas, scientists have learned, are gentle, shy and intelligent. Dr. Richard H. Cohn and Dr. Francine Patterson taught American Sign Language (ASL) to a gorilla named Koko. (ASL is the sign language many deaf people use to communicate.) Over the years, Koko has learned more than 1,000 words. She and a male gorilla companion, Michael, can communicate with the scientists and with each other using ASL. According to Dr. Cohn, "We are learning that gorillas, like humans, are capable of expressing thoughts, feelings, joy and fear." He adds that there are only a few thousand of these gentle creatures left in the world today. He and his colleagues have set up the Gorilla Foundation to find ways to save these and other primates from extinction.

Chimpanzees

Chimpanzees are smaller than gorillas. They have larger brains though, and some scientists think they are more intelligent. Chimps are very playful and curious. They communicate with each other by using their hands, bodies, faces and voice sounds.

Chimps are also very good at learning things and, like Koko the gorilla, some chimps in labs have learned sign language. Scientists are still not sure how much these animals understand of the language and how much is the result of chimps imitating their teachers.

Wild chimps live in forests in Africa. In many of the countries where they live, people want to use the land where the chimps live for farms to grow food. Once millions of chimps ranged through Africa. Now no more than 175,000 remain. Some African countries have started game reserves to protect the chimps and other primates.

Wild chimps live in groups. They sleep in tree nests. They eat fruit, leaves, ants, bird eggs, fish and termites. Jane Goodall observed that they sometimes eat meat. Chimpanzees live from 30 to 38 years in the wild and from 40 to 60 years in zoos and labs.

Primates in Labs

Chimpanzees and other primates are used by scientists for experiments. Some of the experiments have to do with studying how animals learn and communicate. Others have to do with the physical similarities between humans and other primates.

More than 250,000 wild monkeys are used each year for the study of human diseases. Because non-human primates are so similar to people, they often react to diseases, surgery and drugs the same way that people do. If a medical researcher thinks he or she can cure a certain human disease, the scientist might first infect a monkey or other primate with the disease. Then the animal can be given the medicine or treatment to see if it will cure the disease. If it doesn't, there is no risk to the human patient who might have been given the treatment.

Another laboratory use for non-human primates is for experiments in organ transplants. By using primates, doctors can try out different methods without endangering human patients. They experiment on transplanting not only hearts, but also livers, kidneys, lungs and other vital organs using monkeys and other primates.

Doctors use primates to perform valuable medical experiments and save many human lives, but many animals lose their lives in the process.

Some people object to the use of animals in lab experiments because they feel it is cruel and painful for the animals. There are groups that work for strict laws on the care and feeding of laboratory animals and to restrict the kinds of experiments that are performed on them.

An important question about the use of primates in the lab for these kinds of experiments is: Since studying the way primates live and communicate shows how close they are to humans, do they feel emotions in the same kind of way? Jane Goodall thinks so, and she and others are very concerned with the way primates are treated in labs. Scientists disagree on how much primates feel emotion, but some scientists are working on creating better conditions for primates in labs and zoos and keeping the animals as comfortable and happy as possible.

Where to Get
More Information
on Primates

Other Books by Jane Goodall

The Chimpanzees of Gombe: Patterns of Behavior 1986
My Life with the Chimpanzees 1988
The Chimpanzee Family Book 1989
*Through a Window: My Thirty Years with the Chimpanzees
   of Gombe* 1990

Videos

National Geographic specials on apes:
"Monkeys, Apes and Man"
"Miss Goodall and the Wild Chimpanzees"
"Among the Wild Chimpanzees"
"Gorilla"
"Search for the Great Apes"

Photo Books

Koko's Story and *Koko's Kitten* by Francine Patterson,
Scholastic, NY, 1985
Orangutan by Caroline Arnold, Morrow, New York, 1990

Wildlife Organizations

African Wildlife Foundation (AWF)
1717 Massachusetts Ave. NW, Ste. 602
Washington, DC 20036
(202) 265–8393

The Jane Goodall Institute
for Wildlife Research, Education and Conservation
P.O Box 41720
Tucson, AZ 85717
(602) 325–1211

Mountain Gorilla Project
1717 Massachusetts Ave. NW, Ste. 602
Washington, DC 20036
(202) 265–8394

Wildlife Preservation Trust International
34th St. and Girard Ave.
Philadelphia, PA 19104
(215) 222–3634

Wildlife Information Center
629 Green St.
Allentown, PA 18102
(215) 434–1632

Animal Rights Groups

Friends of Animals
Box 1244
Norwalk, CT 06856
(203) 866–5223

Humane Society of the United States
2100 L St. NW
Washington, DC 20037
(202) 452–1100

American Society for the Prevention of Cruelty to
Animals
441 E. 92nd St.
New York, NY 10128
(212) 876–7700

People for the Ethical Treatment of Animals
Box 42516
Washington, DC 20015
(301) 770–7444

Three series of good books for all readers:

Writers' Voices—A multicultural, whole-language series of books offering selections from some of America's finest writers, along with background information, maps, glossaries, questions and activities and many more supplementary materials for readers. Our list of authors includes: Amy Tan • Alex Haley • Alice Walker • Rudolfo Anaya • Louise Erdrich • Oscar Hijuelos • Maxine Hong Kingston • Gloria Naylor • Anne Tyler • Tom Wolfe • Mario Puzo • Avery Corman • Judith Krantz • Larry McMurtry • Mary Higgins Clark • Stephen King • Peter Benchley • Ray Bradbury • Sidney Sheldon • Maya Angelou • Jane Goodall • Mark Mathabane • Loretta Lynn • Katherine Jackson • Carol Burnett • Kareem Abdul-Jabbar • Ted Williams • Ahmad Rashad • Abigail Van Buren • Priscilla Presley • Paul Monette • Robert Fulghum • Bill Cosby • Lucille Clifton • Robert Bly • Robert Frost • Nikki Giovanni • Langston Hughes • Joy Harjo • Edna St. Vincent Millay • William Carlos Williams • Terrence McNally • Jules Feiffer • Alfred Uhry • Horton Foote • Marsha Norman • Lynne Alvarez • Lonne Elder III • ntozake shange • Neil Simon • August Wilson • Harvey Fierstein • Beth Henley • David Mamet • Arthur Miller and Spike Lee.

New Writers' Voices—A series of anthologies and individual narratives by talented new writers. Stories, poems and true life experiences written by adult learners cover such topics as health, home and family, love, work, facing challenges and life in foreign countries. Many *New Writers' Voices* contain photographs and illustrations.

Reference—A reference library for adult new readers and writers. The first two books in the series are *How to Write a Play* and *Discovering Words: The Stories Behind English*.

Write for our free complete catalog:
LVNYC Publishing Program
121 Avenue of the Americas
New York, New York 10013